MASSACHUSETTS

A Picture Book to Remember Her by

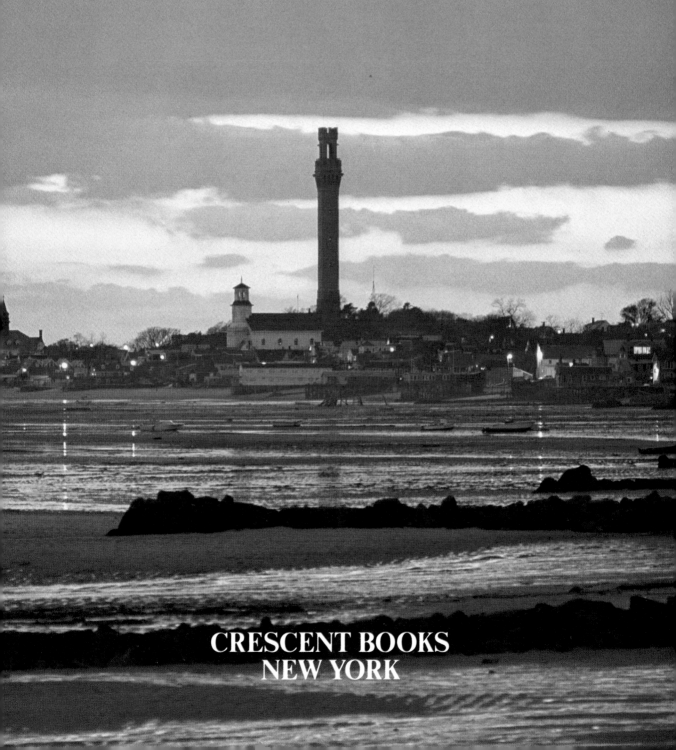

CRESCENT BOOKS
NEW YORK

CLB 1785
© 1987 Illustrations and text: Colour Library Books Ltd.,
    Guildford, Surrey, England.
Text filmsetting by Acesetters Ltd., Richmond, Surrey, England.
Printed and bound in Barcelona, Spain by Cronion, S.A.
All rights reserved.
1987 edition published by Crescent Books, distributed by Crown Publishers, Inc.
ISBN 0 517 62919 4
h g f e d c b a

At least once a year, on Thanksgiving Day, all America is reminded of what we like to call "the Pilgrim Fathers," the people who established the first colony at Plymouth in Massachusetts. In a country without an established aristocracy, generations tried to establish themselves as descendants of the passengers of the Mayflower and, thus, more American than most.

The Pilgrims actually had set sail for Virginia, or at least they said that's where they were going, and claimed to have landed in the wrong place. By having done so, they were free to be independent of the British company that owned Virginia and completely independent of England herself. The rest, as they say, is history.

The history of the United States is preserved in Massachusetts more than anywhere else, especially in the Boston area where the American Revolution began, where the first great stirrings of the Abolitionist movement that led to the Civil War led to lynchings and fiery oratory, where the country's first literary and educational successes let the world know that this was no nation of country bumpkins.

Massachusetts is the state that produced the Adams family and the Kennedy family; it was where the Cabots and the Lowells put an American stamp on the Industrial Revolution. It's the home of Harvard and Amherst and MIT, more universities, in fact than almost any other state. Lexington and Concord, where the War for Independence began, is home today for people who work in one of the world's biggest concentrations of research and electronics facilities.

It's the home of the Boston Symphony and the Boston Pops, of the Berkshire Mountains and hundreds of miles of beautiful beaches. It's quaint little towns and bustling, growing cities. It's Cape Cod and Nantucket and Martha's Vineyard.

For all its rich history, Massachusetts seems right now to be at the peak of its greatness. Though they claimed to be here for religious reasons, the Puritans who established the Massachusetts Bay Colony were hard-headed businessmen and from the very first, their official policies were more oriented toward profit than Puritanism. But religion was important, of course, and when waves of Irish Catholics began arriving after 1845, differences in religion were too important. The old Yankees exploited the newcomers and the newcomers exploited each other.

It is all past history now. Rivalry between ethnic groups has lessened, and though the Massachusetts tradition of individualism is as strong as it ever was, there is more togetherness there now than ever before. And though they like living in small towns and in small houses, the tradition is to think big. And to think young.

Left: churches in Sandwich, the oldest town on the Cape, with Mill Creek Marsh in the foreground.

Among Deerfield's historic buildings are the Memorial Hall (below), displaying Indian and colonial artifacts from the Pocumtuck Valley, and the Dwight-Barnard House (bottom), containing elegant 18th-century furnishings from Boston and the Connecticut Valley. Left: a house at Duxbury. Overleaf: fall in Deerfield, with its restored, 18th-century Ashley House (left).

Above: the First
Congregational Church,
in Williams College
(top and top center),
Williamstown. Above
left: a marina near
Williamstown. Left:
Deerfield Academy,
(far left) Sheldon-
Hawks House, and (top
left) Deerfield Inn,
Deerfield.

Below center: a round stone barn in Hancock Shaker Village (bottom). Below: Upper Sheffield Bridge, Sheffield. Right: the Episcopal Church in Otis (bottom right). Bottom center: Monterey and (far right) the Town Hall in Great Barrington.

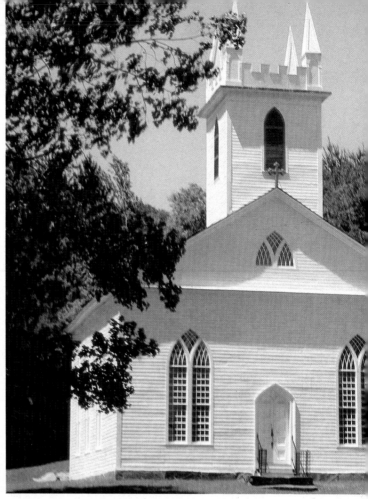

Old Sturbridge Village (these pages), with its pottery (top) and the Pliny Freeman Farm (above and far right), demonstrates facets of early 19th-century life.

Right: Salem Towne House and (bottom center) the Richardson Parsonage stand in Old Sturbridge Village (these pages), as does the 1802 farmhouse (center right) at the Pliny Freeman Farm (far right center).

Above and below left: Battle Green, Lexington. Left: the Meeting House, and (below) a house, in Concord. Facing page: (center left) Barre, and (bottom right) a church at Rockport. Bottom left: the Minuteman Statue, (center right) the Old Manse, and (top left) Old North Bridge, Concord. Top right: a ski-lift, Wachusett Mountain.

Above and right: the shoreline at Little Neck. Facing page: (top left and top right) Rocky Neck, (center left) rowboats at Ipswich, (center right) the harbor at Newburyport, (bottom left) the harborfront at Rockport, and (bottom right) a boardwalk through the Parker River National Wildlife Refuge.

Bottom right: an imposing timbered house in Bass Rocks, and (remaining pictures) the picturesque coastal town of Rockport.

Salem, founded in 1626 and the capital of Massachusetts Bay Colony until 1630, was the setting for the famous witchcraft trials of 1692. By the end of the eighteenth century Salem was a rich maritime port and today displays evidence of its early shipping prowess. Of interest to the visitor in Salem are the newly-constructed Pickering Wharf (left), with its concentration of restaurants and shops, the Jonathan Tanner House (bottom left), and the Custom House (bottom), constructed in 1819 to collect tariff duties, where Nathaniel Hawthorne once worked while surveyor of the port. Facing page: (top left) Manchester Harbor, (center left) boats on the Annisquam River, (top right) the yachting center of Marblehead, and (bottom right, center right and bottom left) boats crowding the harbor at Gloucester, a thriving fishing port.

Many varied styles of architecture
are pleasingly juxtaposed in the city
of Boston (these pages).

Left: Lowell House, Harvard University, and (bottom left) Massachusetts Institute of Technology, Cambridge. Below: the Colonnade Building of the Christian Science Center, (right) the Minuteman Statue, and (bottom center) Massachusetts State House, Boston. Far right: the harbor area, and (bottom right) the Custom House Tower, Boston.

Top: North Bridge, Concord.
Above: the Old State House,
(left) Martha Mary's Chapel, and
(center left and far left)
Merchants Row, Boston (top left).

Boston's buildings, especially those beside water, are transformed by night-time illuminations (these pages).

Above: Duxbury. Top: the Plymouth Rock Memorial, (below) the reconstructed Pilgrim Village, (right) the Massasoit statue, and (far right) a replica of the *Mayflower*, all in Plymouth.

Plymouth (left and top) relives its past in the reconstructed 1627 Pilgrim Village (above left and top left), where costumed staff portray colonial life, and at Jenney Grist Mill (above). Facing page: Duxbury's frozen mid-winter sea.

Cape Cod's changing dune coastline and tidal reaches (these pages) are colored by varying lights.

These pages: small boats, moored (left) at North Falmouth, and (far left) at West Falmouth, on the west coast of Cape Cod. Above: Woods Hole, one of the larger ports of Cape Cod.

Previous pages: (right)
boats grounded on the
sands at low tide
off Provincetown (left).
Above: Nauset Beach, and
(right) the town hall at
Brewster, Cape Cod.
Facing page: (top) the
Highland Light, (bottom)
Chatham Light, and (far
right) Brandt Point Light
guide shipping around
Cape Cod and its islands.

Right: Hyannis Harbor,
(below center) Falmouth
harbor, and (below and
bottom) Dennis, on Cape
Cod. Right: fishing boats
at Provincetown.

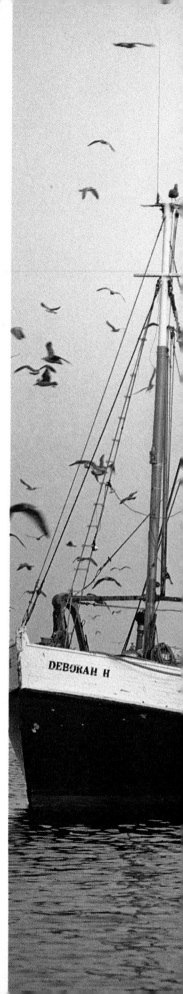

DEBORAH H

The topography of Cape Cod lends itself to the harnessing (above center) of wind power. Left: Brewster Church, Cape Cod. Facing page top left: the 251-foot-high Pilgrim Monument in Provincetown, whose well-preserved inns, shops and houses (remaining pictures) indicate the importance of the summer tourist trade which transforms this fishing town into a vacation resort.

Provincetown (these pages) was
once a thriving whaling port.
Left: a reconstruction of a
captain's quarters and (facing
page) the Town Hall.

49

Facing page bottom: beach
huts along the shore of
Provincetown (remaining
pictures), where fishing is
a major industry.

Top: beach at Provincetown (left).
Above: marshes at Brewster and (above center) near Sandwich. Overleaf: (right) tidal patterns on sand near Brewster, Cape Cod (left).

53

Below, right and facing page bottom: Marconi Beach, South Wellfleet. Bottom: saltmarsh at Harwich, and (facing page top) marina in Barnstable, Cape Cod.

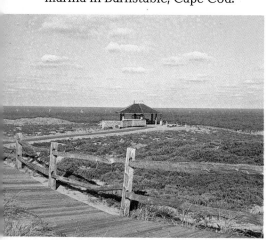

Above: Nashaquista Cliffs at
Gay Head, Martha's Vineyard.
Top: sands of Dionis Beach,
Nantucket Island. Top right:
footprints at Provincelands,
(above right) Race Point
Beach, and (right and facing
page) Marconi Beach, Cape Cod.

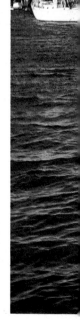

Center left: Nantucket and (remaining pictures) Martha's Vineyard. Far left: Vineyard Haven, (top left) a fishing boat at Dutcher Docks in Menemsha harbor (top and left), and Edgartown Lighthouse (above).

Below and right: Nantucket. Below center right: the ferry *On Time*, connecting Edgartown with Chappaquiddick, where Dyke Bridge (below right) is sited. Remaining pictures and overleaf: the rugged coastline of Martha's Vineyard.